WASHINGTON MIDDLE SCHOOL
314 SOUTH BAIRD STREET
GREEN BAY, WI 54301-3899

OUTDOOR ENCYCLOPEDIAS

THE FISHING ENCYCLOPEDIA

BY DONNA B. MCKINNEY

Encyclopedias

An Imprint of Abdo Reference
abdobooks.com

TABLE OF CONTENTS

HISTORY OF FISHING

Fishing has been popular since ancient times. Historians have found records of people fishing with bamboo rods more than 4,000 years ago. Images of people fishing appear on carvings in tombs and in paintings on vases. The ancient Greeks, Romans, Egyptians, Macedonians, and Chinese all left records describing fishing. These ancient peoples used hooks, nets, and harpoons to catch the fish. American Indians who lived near the Pacific coast in what is now California, including the Coast Miwok, fished. They made hooks from bone and wood.

Ancient Egyptian wall paintings from the 1300s BCE show people fishing with spears.

People continue to smoke fish for the rich flavor the smoke gives the meat.

The first people who fished did so to feed themselves and their families. Without modern conveniences like refrigerators to store the fish, they ate the fish right away. As time passed, people learned to keep fish longer by preserving it through drying, salting, or smoking. People started catching large quantities of fish to sell. Their methods of fishing improved, as did their ways of keeping the fish fresh until they reached the marketplace. The commercial fishing industry began to grow.

DID YOU KNOW?

Scientists who study fossils believe fish have been on Earth for more than 500 million years. A fish fossil called *Metaspriggina walcotti* was found in Canada. This small fish fossil is about 518 million years old.

Fishing remains an important part of life for many American Indian nations, including the Yupik.

In North America, Indigenous people across the continent had been fishing long before Europeans arrived. Commercial fishing started in North America in the early 1500s. By the time of the Revolutionary War (1775–1783), commercial fishing was an important industry in what is now the United States. As technology advanced, fewer people had to fish for food. But they continued to fish for enjoyment. This is called recreational

fishing or sport fishing. In recreational fishing, people might fish strictly for fun or to compete in tournaments. They might keep the fish they catch and eat them. Or they might set them free—a practice called catch and release.

Artists have painted scenes of people fishing throughout history, including this 1800s work from the United States.

AN ACTIVITY FOR ALL AGES

Recreational fishing is one of the most popular outdoor activities in the United States. And it continues to grow. The 2020 Special Report on Fishing gathered data on fishing in the United States during 2019. In that year, 50.1 million people ages six and older fished at least one time. Freshwater fishing is the most popular type of fishing. Saltwater fishing comes in second, and fly-fishing is third.

Fishing is an activity that is accessible to people of all ages. Kids, parents, and grandparents can all enjoy fishing.

The fishing opener, which is the day a state's fishing season begins, can attract a lot of people to popular fishing spots.

Parents or grandparents who enjoy fishing can teach their children and grandchildren to love the hobby too.

The 2020 Special Report on Fishing states that in 2019, 91 percent of the people fishing started during childhood. Fishing is a hobby that is passed down through generations.

Fishing is just one of many ways to enjoy the outdoors. Anglers, or people who fish, often participate in other outdoor activities, such as camping or hiking.

URBAN FISHING

Many people enjoy fishing in rural spaces far from town. But some people fish in cities too. Urban fishing takes place in canals, lakes, rivers, or ponds found in cities. Some cities support urban fishing programs. They stock their ponds and lakes with fish and encourage fishing in these waters.

Some people slowly grow their collections of fishing tackle over many years.

GETTING STARTED

Fishing gear is called tackle. As with many hobbies or sports, tackle can be an expensive investment. But anglers can start fishing with just a few basic pieces of tackle, such as a rod and reel with some line and a hook on it. Other essential items in a beginner's tackle box might include weights, lures, a small knife or scissors, and needle-nose pliers. A person who is new to fishing could get started by borrowing tackle or spending money on just a few items.

Fish are found in lakes, rivers, ponds, streams, and the ocean. Most people in the United States are near a fishing spot. A license is needed for most fishing in the United States. Requirements vary by state, so people should look up the local licensing requirements that apply to them. After that, they can get ready to fish.

There are many places people can go to catch fish.

FRESHWATER FISHING

Great freshwater fishing is found across the United States. Fresh water has little or no salt. In the United States, fresh water might include rivers, lakes, streams, ponds, creeks,

People fish in lakes across the country, including at Lake Winnipesaukee in New Hampshire.

People may fish for food in fresh water while camping.

or reservoirs. In 2019, more than 39 million people in the United States went freshwater fishing. There are many types of tackle that can help make a freshwater fishing trip successful.

EYE

ROD

LINE

REEL

The fishing rod is the base to which several pieces of equipment are attached.

RODS

A rod is one of the most important pieces of fishing equipment. It is a long, slightly flexible stick. Other fishing equipment attaches to the rod.

The spinning rod, also called the spin rod, is among the most common freshwater rods. On this rod, the reel of fishing line hangs down from the handle. Mounted on the underside of the rod are the guides, or eyes. These are the small metal circles that the line runs through. Spinning rods are typically made of graphite or fiberglass. These rods range in length from 5 to 8.5 feet (1.5 to 2.6 m). The reels for spinning rods are held in place with a sliding lock that allows the angler to easily remove the reel. The spinning rod is best suited for fishing in lakes or rivers, as well as fishing from boats. These rods are used to catch a wide range of fish, including trout, bass, pike, and walleye.

The spinning rod is a versatile rod.

The casting rod is fairly similar to the spinning rod.

The casting rod is another type of freshwater rod. The main difference between the casting rod and the spinning rod is the location of the reel. On the casting rod, the reel and the eyes attach to the rod above the handle.

The telescoping rod is small and lightweight. It can be a great rod to carry when camping or backpacking. Sections of the rod screw together. When the screws are loosened, the rod can be shortened for easy carrying. A telescoping rod as long as 30 feet (9.1 m) can be collapsed to about 1.5 feet (0.5 m) long. Like the spinning and casting rods, these rods are made of graphite or fiberglass.

The telescoping rod is made in segments that can each be collapsed into the segment before it.

REELS

The reel attaches to the rod and holds the fishing line. An angler can spin the handle to bring in the fishing line and wrap it back around the spool. The spinning rod uses a spinning reel. There is no cover over the spool, so the

SPOOL

BAIL

When the bail is closed on a spinning reel, it arcs around the spool.

When a spinning reel's bail is open, it arcs up over the top of the spool.

fishing line can be easily seen. Spinning reels are sometimes called open-face reels or open-bail reels. The spinning reel has a bail, which is a heavy metal wire. The bail can be moved back and forth from a locked, or closed, position to an open position. Opening the bail allows fishing line to run off the spool. Closing the bail prevents any more line from unreeling. Learning how to open and close the bail when casting takes a little practice. But with practice, even a beginner can easily learn to fish with this kind of reel.

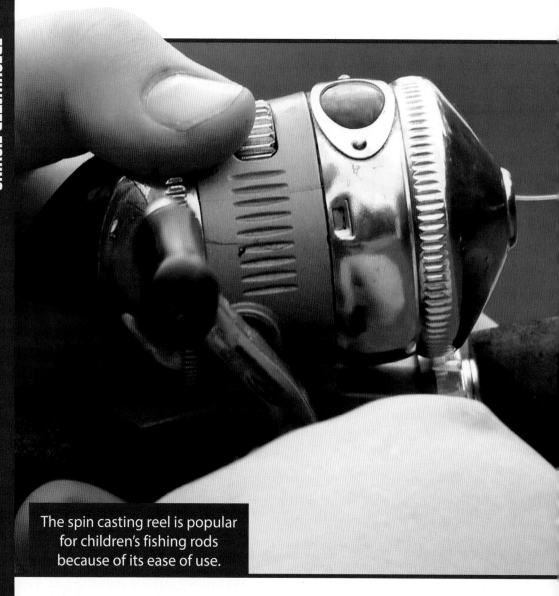

The spin casting reel is popular for children's fishing rods because of its ease of use.

The casting rod typically uses a closed spin casting reel. This reel is considered the easiest for a beginner. The reel mounts above the rod handle. It has a protective cover. Unlike the spinning reel, there is no bail to handle while casting. To release the fishing line, the angler simply releases a button on the reel.

The bait-casting reel allows the angler to cast heavier lures or bait at greater distances. These reels are mounted above the rod handle. Bait-casting reels are more complex to use than spinning reels or closed spin casting reels. They take more practice to use well.

Like other types of reels, most bait-casting reels have the crank on the right side, but some are made for left-handed people too.

FISHING LINE

The rod and reel help with the support and use of the line. Anglers use three basic types of fishing line. These are monofilament, fluorocarbon, and braided. Monofilament line is typically a single strand of nylon. It comes in a variety of colors. Monofilament line is popular for beginners. It is relatively inexpensive and easy to tie in knots. Because monofilament line stretches a bit, some more experienced anglers prefer other lines. That stretch makes it a little harder for the angler to feel a fish nibbling on the bait.

A sturdy knot is important for catching fish, so beginners often favor monofilament as they learn to tie fishing knots.

Some people use line crimps instead of knots, especially for heavy line that doesn't hold a knot well.

While monofilament is the most popular type of fishing line, fluorocarbon line is gaining popularity. Some anglers who fish in very clear waters like this line because it is almost invisible. Fluorocarbon is a single strand line like monofilament. But it is made from different chemical compounds, so it is thinner than monofilament lines of the same strength. Fluorocarbon line does not stretch as much as monofilament and is more durable. Tying knots with this line can be a little more difficult because it is stiffer than monofilament or braided lines.

Because braiding makes line stronger, a braided line will be able to handle a heavier fish than another line of the same diameter.

Braided line is made from fibers of polyethylene braided together. It is stronger than fluorocarbon or monofilament line. It can be more difficult to tie in knots than monofilament line, but easier than fluorocarbon line. Household nail clippers can cut monofilament and fluorocarbon line. But scissors are needed to cut the stronger braided line. Because braided line has no stretch, it can be easier for the angler to feel the fish nibbling on the bait.

DID YOU KNOW?

Rods and reels are often sold separately, allowing anglers to choose the best rod and the best reel for their fishing plans. For beginners, a rod and reel purchased in combination can be a smart choice. In this case, the rod, reel, and fishing line already on the spool are sold as one item.

Anglers often choose which line to use based on the line's strength, which is called test. The fishing line strength is measured in pound test, which is also called line test. The pound test describes how much weight would cause the line to snap. For example, a 6-pound (2.7 kg) test line should be capable of landing a 6-pound (2.7 kg) fish without breaking. A 30-pound (14 kg) test line should be able to land a 30-pound (14 kg) fish without breaking.

The fishing line's package will say what pound test the line is.

Anglers may keep several different hook sizes.

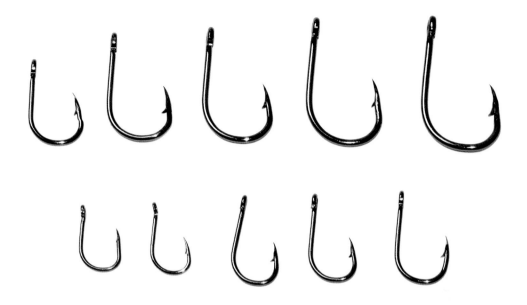

Knowing the size of the species being fished will help an angler select an appropriate hook size.

HOOKS

A hook attaches to the end of the line. Hooks might also be described by size. Generally the size is described by a number, with size 32 being the smallest hook and 1 being the largest hook. There is a second numbering system for hooks that ranges from 1/0 to 19/0. With this second numbering system, the larger number matches to the larger hook. Anglers typically choose the hook size based on the size of the fish they are trying to catch. If the hook is too small, a big fish might swallow both the bait and hook. If the hook is too large, a small fish cannot bite it. Choosing the right hook size is important for fishing success.

Hooks come in different shapes. The hook can also be described based on its purpose, such as a bait-cast hook or spin-cast hook. A common hook shape is the J hook, shaped like the letter *J*. The J hook has been used by generations of anglers. It remains popular today, especially for beginners. Some anglers use round hooks called circle hooks, especially when catching and releasing fish. It is easier to unhook and release the fish and causes less damage to the fish's mouth.

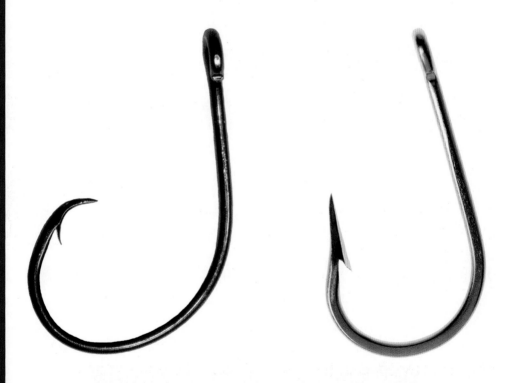

The circle hook, *left*, is more likely to hook the fish's mouth and less likely to hook deep in the gut, so it does less damage than the J hook, *right*.

Fish get hooked when they try to eat bait.

BAIT

Anglers sometimes attract fish by attaching bait to the hooks. Bait is typically an animal or part of an animal that fish might eat. Freshwater baits come in all shapes and sizes. Some states have regulations about the use of live baits. These regulations can usually be found on a state's fish and wildlife website.

The wriggling motion of a worm attracts many types of fish.

Worms are a commonly used freshwater bait. Worms can be easily found by digging with a shovel in a garden or shaded area of a yard. Tackle and bait shops also sell worms for fishing. Earthworms and nightcrawlers are good for catching walleye and bass. Small manure worms found in cow or horse pastures are good for catching trout or panfish such as sunfish. Grubs and mealworms are also good for catching trout, sunfish, or panfish.

Cut bait is a fish cut into pieces and used as the bait to catch a bigger fish. Some anglers will catch a small fish, such as a perch, bluegill, sunfish, herring, or shad, to cut up and use as bait. The scent from the cut bait attracts the larger fish. Cut bait is popular for catching catfish and carp.

WHAT IS A PANFISH?

Anglers sometimes talk about fishing for panfish. The word *panfish* does not refer to a specific species of fish. It typically describes any small fish that fits in a frying pan. They include sunfish, crappies, bluegills, and perch. Beginning anglers often enjoy fishing for panfish. They are usually plentiful and easy to catch.

Small fish can be cut up and frozen to use later, or they can be used on the same outing.

Anglers keep minnows in an insulated container that protects them from extreme temperatures.

Dough balls are small balls of dough molded around the hook. They are a mixture of flour, cornmeal, sugar, water, and molasses. Fish such as trout, catfish, carp, and panfish all eat dough-ball bait. Tackle and bait shops sell dough balls. Some anglers make their own. A variety of recipes can be found online.

The hook should go down the middle of the grasshopper's body lengthwise.

Minnows are another popular freshwater bait. These tiny fish are alive when the angler places them on the hook. They can be purchased at tackle and bait shops. Some anglers catch their own minnows using nets. Anglers use live minnows to catch trout, pike, bass, stripers, crappies, and bluegills.

Crickets and grasshoppers are a good bait when fishing for sunfish or other panfish. Tackle or bait shops sell these insects. Some anglers catch their own by searching in grassy areas or under rocks and logs.

Crayfish are also used as bait. They can be either alive or dead. Anglers use live crayfish to catch smallmouth bass. They use dead crayfish to catch catfish or carp. Crayfish are sold at tackle and bait shops.

LURES

Lures are artificial bait made to look and move like a fish's prey. They can be used instead of or with real bait. A jig is a colorful lure with a metal head and some sort of tail. The tail piece is typically made of rubber, plastic, feathers, or animal hair. The hook is hidden in the tail. Some anglers also attach bait to the hook. The jig's head is weighted so when the angler casts this lure, it sinks. Then the angler lifts up the rod tip a little, reels in some line, and then lets it drop to the bottom again. The angler continues to repeat these movements to attract a fish. This kind of fishing is called jigging.

Some jigs look like grubs.

Although most plugs have two treble hooks, they can have other hook arrangements too.

Plugs are lures made to look like small baitfish or frogs. They are typically made of plastic or wood with two treble hooks attached to the lure. A treble hook is a cluster of three hooks extending from a single center. Plugs are also called crankbaits, wobblers, shallow-divers, or deep-divers. Anglers allow plugs to sink down into the water and then reel in the lure, hoping to attract a fish.

Soft plastic lures look like small, colorful worms, frogs, minnows, shrimp, or crayfish. A soft plastic lure sometimes has a built-in weight attached to it. The weight makes it easier to cast into the water. Some plastic lures have a scent that is attractive to fish. Soft plastic lures can be purchased either with or without the hook embedded in them. When the lure does not come with a hook already attached, the angler threads the soft lure onto a hook. Anglers trying to catch bass frequently use soft plastic lures.

Soft plastic lures may have loose strips that make it seem like the back legs are moving.

The spinner is a flat blade, *yellow*, that is hooked up to the rest of the lure.

A spinnerbait lure consists of a wire frame, a weight, spinner blades, and a hook. Anglers used to call them safety-pin lures because the wire frames look like open safety pins. The hook is usually covered by animal hair, feathers, or soft rubber streamers. When pulled through the water, the spinnerbait's blades flash and move like a tiny fish swimming through the water. This lure is often used to catch largemouth and smallmouth bass, pike, or walleye.

DID YOU KNOW?

Some fishing lures vibrate. These lures are made of plastic or metal with a tiny motor inside. When the angler reels in the lure, the motor vibrates to attract fish.

A spoon lure is cupped.

A spoon lure looks a bit like a tablespoon. It is made of metal with a hook attached to one end. As the angler reels in the line, the spoon moves through the water like a minnow. The design is intended to look like an injured baitfish. Anglers like to use spoons for a variety of fish, including trout, pike, perch, salmon, walleye, largemouth bass, and muskellunge, which are often called muskies.

Surface lures are lures that anglers reel in quickly across the top of the water. They often look like small, colorful baitfish. Surface lures usually have one or two treble hooks attached to the body. Surface lures have various names depending on how they work in the water. A stickbait is one type. The angler uses the rod to jerk this lure across the top of the water. The wobbly, splashing lure looks like an injured baitfish. It attracts the attention of larger fish such as bass, pike, or muskies.

Surface baits are made of material that floats or sinks only a little.

The propbait is another surface lure. This lure has tiny propellors that create a buzzing noise when pulled through the water. Anglers also use these for catching bass, pike, and muskies. Poppers are yet another kind of surface lure. The face of these lures is concave, or angled inward. When the angler retrieves the lure quickly, it makes a popping or splashing sound as it moves through the water. As the lure splashes along on the water's surface, it looks like an injured frog or small fish. Poppers are often used for catching bass, trout, and panfish.

The propbait has a propeller at the front and at the back of the lure.

A popping lure often looks like a fish with its mouth open.

OTHER TACKLE

Besides these main pieces of tackle, there is other gear that can make a fishing day a success. One is the leader. The regular fishing line is lightweight enough that it can be easily cut by a fish's mouth or the rough parts of its body. Anglers often fasten a fishing leader between the end of the fishing line and the hook or the lure. This short length of heavy-duty fishing line or wire gives extra protection against the line breaking once a fish is hooked.

Many kinds of bait float on top of the water. A weight, also called a sinker, is a piece of metal tied to the end of the fishing line. The weight causes bait to sink and reach deeper fish. Most weights are made of lead. Some people are concerned that lead weights might contribute to lead poisoning in wildlife. Affected animals may lose their appetite, show confusion, and even die. So some states restrict the use of lead fishing weights. Substitutes include weights made of steel or the metals tin or tungsten.

Weights range from pieces about the size of a small pea to heavy weights about the size of a baseball. Weights also come in various shapes, including tear-shaped, flat or oval, pyramid-shaped, and pencil-shaped. Some weights are tied to the fishing line. Other weights are pinched onto the line using a pair of pliers. Lures can also have weights built in, such as a small weight with a plastic worm or grub attached to it.

The split shot weight has a slit in the middle. This weight is pinched onto fishing line with pliers.

Weights are needed for fish that live in deeper water.

Bobbers are bright colors so they are easy to see at a distance.

Fishing bobbers, also called floats, attach to the line and float on top of the water. Some bobbers slide along the line. Others are attached to a certain spot on the line. These keep the bait from sinking beyond a certain depth. The colorful bobber floats on top of the water. When the bobber is pulled underwater, it signals the angler that a fish has grabbed the bait.

Two other pieces of fishing tackle are snaps and swivels. Snaps look like safety pins. Anglers tie them to the ends of their fishing lines. Snaps allows anglers to quickly attach and remove items like leaders, lures, or hooks. The swivel is another item an angler might tie to the end of the line. Swivels are small fasteners with two or more tiny rings, called eyes, that can spin around. The line attaches to one end, and the leader or the lure is fastened to the other. The swivel helps keep the lure and line from getting twisted and tangled while moving through the water.

The swivel allows the lure and line to twist in opposite directions.

The amount of small fishing tackle items available for the angler might seem overwhelming. For the beginning angler, having a more experienced angler to help guide the shopping can be helpful. In addition, the people who work in fishing tackle stores are often anglers themselves. They can be good resources for beginning anglers trying to decide what tackle to purchase.

Anglers can see and feel some tools in person at tackle stores. This helps them find the best products for their needs.

There are many styles of tackle boxes to choose from.

TACKLE BOX

With all the pieces of gear an angler needs, a tackle box is a handy way to carry gear to a fishing spot. Tackle boxes are often made of hard plastic, with several trays inside to keep the gear organized. But soft-sided tackle bags are available as well. These tackle bags hold several plastic boxes where the fishing tackle items are stored. Both types have plenty of small compartments for holding the hooks, lures, weights, and other items an angler needs.

Anglers may prefer tackle boxes that can make most of their gear easily accessible at once.

When choosing a tackle box or bag, anglers look for sturdy handles, a secure fastener or latch, and plenty of roomy compartments for the gear. A tackle box or bag can be very heavy to carry. So while it might be tempting to buy a large tackle box, buyers should remember that the box must be carried to the pond, lake, or river and back. One advantage of the tackle bag is that anglers can choose which plastic boxes to carry on a fishing trip and which to leave at home, lightening the load in the bag.

WHERE TO GO FRESHWATER FISHING

Freshwater anglers have plenty of waters to choose from. Lakes, reservoirs, ponds, rivers, and streams are located across the United States. No matter where an angler is fishing, he or she should learn what permits might be needed before heading out to fish. This information is usually found on a state's fish and wildlife website.

People often fish from the shore of a lake.

Fishing can happen from the shore, a dock, a pier, or a boat. Some bodies of water are located on public land, while others are on private property. Anglers must get permission from

Fishing from a boat can give anglers access to species that live only in deep water.

Ice fishing augers can be motorized or driven by hand.

the owner before fishing on private land. Fishing is allowed on state and national park lands. However, there can be special regulations that apply, so it is wise to check with park rangers before fishing. Online fishing forums for the area can help anglers find the best spots to catch a fish.

DID YOU KNOW?

Ice fishing takes place on frozen lakes and ponds. Anglers use a tool called an auger to make a large hole in the ice over a frozen lake or pond. They fish through that hole, catching fish such as pike, crappies, and bass.

Tackle store employees can help anglers select tackle.

HOW TO CATCH FRESHWATER FISH

Many experienced anglers post instructional videos online. These videos can help an inexperienced angler learn specific fishing skills, such as tying knots or removing a fish from the hook. Tackle and bait stores are good places to ask questions.

Beginners may also choose to learn from an experienced angler. Many anglers are happy to share their knowledge with beginners.

Experienced anglers may go fishing with newer anglers and teach them while they fish.

For beginners, casting the line is likely one of the most challenging skills. New anglers can practice casting in an open area outside without trees in front of them. They can tie

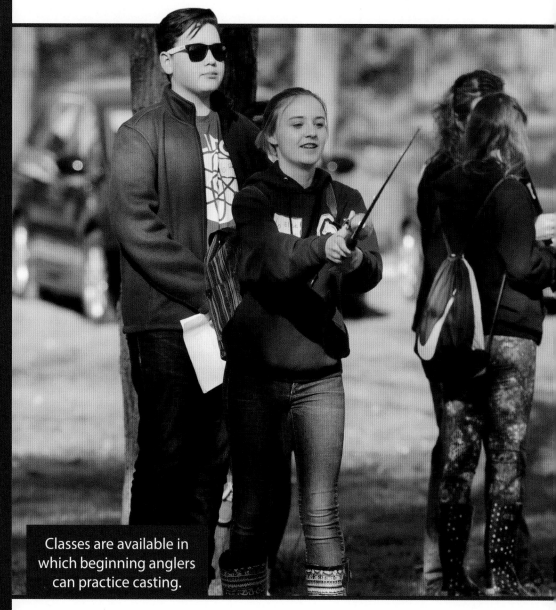

Classes are available in which beginning anglers can practice casting.

Having an accurate cast can be important for fishing in crowded and wooded areas.

weights without hooks on the ends of their lines. Then they can start casting. To become more accurate, they can practice casting the weight into large buckets or boxes. With some practice, an inexperienced angler can gain confidence and skill before arriving at the water.

GREAT FISHING LAKES

Take Me Fishing is a nonprofit organization dedicated to increasing participation in recreational fishing. It also helps conserve the United States' natural resources. In 2021, Take Me Fishing chose its top ten fishing lakes in the United States. Its recommended lakes were Grand Lake, Colorado; Mille Lacs Lake, Minnesota; Lake Istokpoga, Florida; Sam Rayburn Reservoir, Texas; Lake Fork, Texas; Lake Winnipesaukee, New Hampshire; Clear Lake, California; Lake of the Woods, Minnesota; Big Green Lake, Wisconsin; and Hubbard Lake, Michigan.

When the fish pulls the bobber underwater, the hook is ready to be set.

The next skill to think about is setting the hook. *Setting the hook* is the term that describes the action of getting the fish onto the hook. This technique requires patience and attention to the details of what is happening with the line. Fish often bump or nibble a bait before actually grabbing hold of it. When this is happening, the angler may feel just gentle taps on the line. If the angler is using a bobber, likely the bobber will start moving up and down in the water. Once the bobber is pulled completely under the water or there is a strong tug on the line, the angler gives a strong pull up on the rod, lifting the rod tip high. This motion needs to be a strong pull to be sure the hook is securely set in the fish's mouth.

Fish will try to swim away once the hook is set, pulling against the line.

If the fish is hooked, the angler should be able to feel the fish's weight on the line. Sometimes a fish is hooked or seems to be hooked but then shakes itself free. This happens to even the most experienced anglers at times. With the fish firmly hooked, the angler reels the fish in until it is close to the dock,

Anglers can pull some fish out of the water on the line.

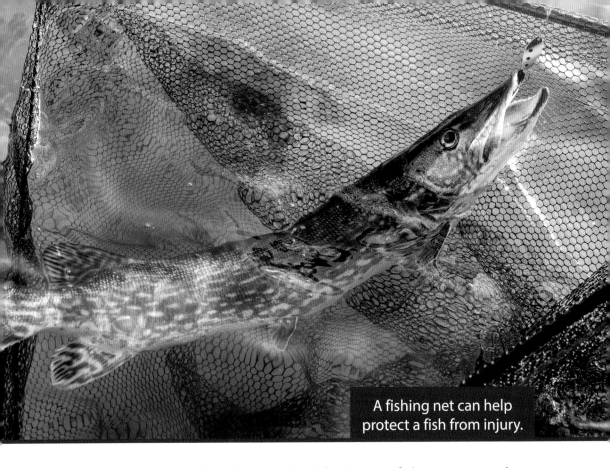

A fishing net can help protect a fish from injury.

shore, or boat. Smaller fish can be lifted out of the water and onto the dock, shore, or boat. Some anglers scoop out larger fish with a fishing net. If anglers are fishing to catch and release the fish, they will move quickly to remove the hook as gently as possible and then slip the fish back into the water. Many anglers recommend using a net when the plan is to release the fish. It is healthier for the fish not to be handled too much. Using a net cuts down on the handling. Fishing gloves are also useful for the angler who is catching and releasing. The gloves protect the angler's hands from a fish's teeth and spines. If anglers are keeping the fish, they generally store it in a container filled with water, called a live well, until they can get it home for cleaning and cooking.

FRESHWATER FISH SPECIES

Anglers enjoy catching many different types of fish.

Freshwater anglers have a variety of fish species they can catch. Some are known for putting up a thrilling fight on the end of the line, while others are prized for their flavor. Anglers should find out which species live in the planned fishing spot and which they would like to catch. This will influence the tackle used.

BLUEGILLS

The bluegill is also called the sunny, bream, brim, sun perch, and copper belly. It is in the sunfish family. The bluegill gets its name from the bluish color on its cheek and gill cover. This fish is native to the eastern United States but is now found in other parts of the country. It lives in lakes, ponds, rivers, streams, and reservoirs.

The bluegill's body is flat, and its color varies from dark blue to olive green to yellow. It has several dark vertical stripes on its body. The heaviest bluegills caught weigh nearly 5 pounds (2.3 kg). They are usually about 7.5 inches (19 cm) long. Worms and night crawlers are common bait for catching bluegills.

A bluegill is just one of many sunfish species, which are common catches in North America.

CATFISH

More than 40 different catfish species live in North America. The channel catfish, blue catfish, and bullhead are some of the most popular catfish with anglers. Catfish do not have scales on their bodies like most other fish. But they do have taste buds all over their bodies. So some people call the catfish a swimming tongue. Catfish have barbels that look like

Bullheads are easy fish to catch.

The blue catfish can be caught with live or artificial bait.

cat whiskers around their mouths. These barbels help them find their food.

The blue catfish is among the biggest US catfish species. This fish is bluish-gray in color and has a white belly. The blue catfish can reach nearly 5 feet (1.5 m) long and can weigh more than 100 pounds (45 kg). It is found mainly in the southeastern United States, but it also lives in California. The channel catfish can be olive to light blue in color with black specks along its sides. Fishing after dark usually brings anglers the best luck in catching channel catfish.

A male salmon's jaws develop a hooked shape when he moves from salt water to fresh water.

CHINOOK SALMON

Chinook salmon are also called the king salmon, spring salmon, and blackmouth. They are found along the US Pacific coast. Chinook are anadromous, meaning they live in salt water but travel to fresh water to breed. In the ocean, the Chinook is a blue-green color with silver-white sides and belly. Its gums and mouth are black. In fresh waters when spawning, the Chinook changes color to become olive brown, purple, or red.

Chinook are the largest of the Pacific coast salmon. These fish can grow to be about 5 feet (1.5 m) long and weigh more than 120 pounds (54 kg). Alaska is a great place to fish for salmon. Five Pacific salmon species—Chinook, coho, sockeye, pink, and chum salmon—live in Alaska's waters. Summer is the best time to fish for salmon in Alaska.

Salmon is a popular fish to eat.

Black crappie

CRAPPIES

Both black crappies and white crappies are found in the United States. Sometimes anglers confuse the two fish because their coloring is similar. Both fish have dark-olive or black coloring with silver on the sides. Both fish also have patterns of spots on their sides. But the patterns are different. The black crappie's spots are irregular shapes. The white crappie's spots are neatly arranged into vertical stripes.

Both black and white crappies are found across much of the United States. Crappies can grow to be 1 foot (0.3 m) long and weigh about 4 pounds (1.8 kg). Some anglers like to use a small spinnerbait or a live minnow when fishing for crappies. These fish tend to hide around submerged trees.

White crappie

LARGEMOUTH BASS

The largemouth bass can be found in every US state. It also goes by the names black bass, green bass, green trout, and Florida bass. This greenish fish has a dark horizontal stripe along its body. The heaviest largemouth bass ever caught in the United States weighed slightly more than 22 pounds (10 kg).

The largemouth bass is named for its mouth, which can open very wide.

Largemouth bass often jump out of the water when hooked.

The largemouth bass is one of the most popular freshwater fish to catch. It is a smart fish and can see a lure and learn to avoid it. In some lakes where fishing is heavy, these fish have learned to avoid most of the commonly used lures. Bass use their sharp eyesight to hunt for their food. So the best time to catch them is when the sunlight is not so bright. Just after sunrise and just before dark can be good times to fish for largemouth bass.

The muskie can put up a good fight when hooked.

MUSKELLUNGE

The muskellunge is commonly called the muskie. This fish has a long, narrow body and a mouth shaped like a duck bill. The muskie has a silver body with a white belly. Dark-colored spots or stripes cover its body. These fish live in the northern and northeastern parts of the United States.

Sometimes muskies are called the "fish of 10,000 casts" because they are so hard to catch. The nickname suggests it could take 10,000 casts of the fishing line to land a muskie. They are fast fish, able to swim at speeds of 30 miles per hour (48 kmh). The largest muskellunge ever caught in the United States weighed more than 67 pounds (30 kg) and was slightly more than 5 feet (1.5 m) long. In lakes, muskellunge swim near thick weed beds, so anglers fish near where deeper water begins and the weed bed ends. This area is called a break line.

Muskies are difficult to catch because they can be unpredictable in their hunting and feeding habits.

NORTHERN PIKE

The northern pike is a Holarctic species, which means it can live in Arctic waters in addition to other northern waters. In the United States, the northern pike is found in lakes, ponds, and rivers across the West, Midwest, and Northeast. Other names include great northern pickerel, jack, jackfish, and northern. This fish is similar in appearance to the muskie.

The northern has a long, narrow body and a mouth shaped like a duck's bill. Its colors are greenish and yellowish, with oblong-shaped spots on the sides of its body. While many fish

Although the northern looks similar to the muskie, the northern typically has light spots, while the muskie has dark stripes or spots.

A large northern is an exciting catch for anglers.

have two dorsal fins, the northern is easy to spot because it has only a single dorsal fin located near its tail. This fish is the top predator in the waters where it lives. With needle-sharp teeth, it is a quick, aggressive feeder that eats smaller fish, frogs, small mammals, birds, and crayfish. The northern can grow to be 4.6 feet (1.4 m) long and can weigh 46 pounds (21 kg). Anglers keep their fingers away from the northern pike's mouth when removing the hook or lure to avoid being bitten.

The smallmouth bass is one of the strongest freshwater fish for its size.

SMALLMOUTH BASS

The smallmouth bass, also called the black bass, is related to the largemouth bass, but it doesn't grow as large. The smallmouth bass can weigh almost 12 pounds (5.4 kg). Compared with the largemouth bass, the smallmouth is typically more brownish in color while the largemouth is more greenish. The smallmouth also has vertical stripes on its body. This bass prefers fast-flowing streams and deeper pools of water. Live minnows, spinnerbaits, and plugs are some of the favorite baits and lures for smallmouth bass fishing. These fish hide in water where there is cover. Anglers fish for them in waters where there are overhanging trees, weed beds, or large rocks.

FRESHWATER FISH IN HAWAII

The Hawaiian Islands are famous for their saltwater fish. They have plenty of freshwater streams and reservoirs as well. However, there are only two freshwater fish native to Hawaii. These fish are the goby and the eleotrid. But game fish like the largemouth bass, channel catfish, rainbow trout, and smallmouth bass have been introduced to Hawaii's waters and thrive there. Panfish are plentiful in the reservoirs.

Smallmouth bass often put up a better fight than largemouth bass.

STEELHEAD

A trout called the steelhead is another popular fish to catch. Some steelhead live in fresh water all their lives. These are called rainbow trout. Other steelhead migrate to salty ocean waters and return to fresh waters to spawn. This trout is native to the western coast of North America, from Alaska to Mexico. It has been introduced in other parts of the United States and is now found in many states.

A rainbow trout

A steelhead

This trout has a broad, red-pink stripe along its side. While steelhead can grow to be nearly 50 pounds (23 kg), they are typically around 8 pounds (3.6 kg). The steelhead is one of four major trout species found in the United States. The other three are the brook trout, cutthroat trout, and brown trout. Anglers fish for steelhead in shore areas with boulders or large rocks. The fish often hide around the rocks.

Striped bass can live up to 30 years.

STRIPED BASS

The striped bass also goes by the names striper, rockfish, and greenhead. These fish are anadromous. This silver-white bass has horizontal black stripes running along its body. These fish are usually 1 to 3 feet (0.3 to 0.9 m) long and weigh 2 to 20 pounds (0.9 to 9 kg), though they can be up to 80 pounds (36 kg).

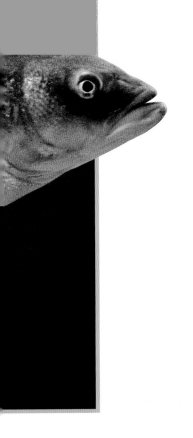

This fish is found in the eastern United States, along the Gulf coast, and along the Atlantic coast. Some striped bass migrate. Those that live in states such as North Carolina, Virginia, or Maryland travel to the Atlantic ocean and up the coast to northern waters in the summer and then return to those states when summer ends. Other striped bass live in large freshwater river systems and never migrate. These fish feed at low-light times of day. Anglers fish for striped bass at dawn, at dusk, or after dark.

The striped bass is Maryland's state fish.

WALLEYE

The walleye is also called the pike perch, walleyed pickerel, yellow pike, and walleye pike. It is the largest member of the perch family. The walleye is mostly gold and olive with black stripes across its back. This fish gets its name from its large, glassy-looking eyes.

Walleye are most active at night, so dawn and dusk can be good times to fish for them.

A bait and lure combination can be helpful for catching walleye.

Walleye feed at night, which makes sunrise and sunset the best times to fish for them. They can grow to be about 3 feet (0.9 m) long and weigh up to 20 pounds (9 kg). The walleye is found in the northern, western, and northeastern parts of the United States. A walleye's diet is mostly smaller fish. An angler may use a minnow or a lure that imitates a minnow for bait. The walleye is a popular fish to eat.

WHITE STURGEONS

White sturgeons are the largest freshwater fish in North America. The biggest sturgeon on record, caught in 1898, weighed about 1,500 pounds (680 kg). Sturgeons are found in waters along the western coast of the United States.

The sturgeon does not have scales on its body like most fish. Instead, it has rows of bony plates, called scutes, covering

White sturgeons can live for more than 100 years.

Sturgeons don't typically swim away with the bait, so an angler needs to pay attention to the small tugs so he or she can set the hook when a sturgeon has it in its mouth.

its skin. These scutes can be very sharp. Sturgeons do not have teeth. Instead, they use their mouths like a vacuum cleaner to suck in food. The fish has barbels that look like whiskers on its snout. Sturgeons are anadromous. They are born in large freshwater rivers near the coast. Some sturgeons swim to salt water, while others spend their whole lives in fresh water. Sturgeons keep growing as long as they live. Anglers fishing for sturgeons use bait like grass shrimp, night crawlers, or chunks of lamprey, smelt, or shad.

SALTWATER FISHING

Piers are popular places to go saltwater fishing.

With its long Atlantic, Pacific, and Gulf coasts, the United States offers plenty of saltwater fishing. Alaska and Hawaii also provide great saltwater fishing spots. Saltwater fishing takes place in waters that have some salt content. This includes the ocean waters along the US coast. It also includes the bays and rivers near the coast. They are salty because they are so near the ocean. In 2019, more than 13 million people in the United States went saltwater fishing. Whether fishing from a pier, in the surf, on a boat, or on quieter inshore waters, saltwater fishing offers plenty of excitement for anglers.

The tackle for saltwater fishing is similar to that for freshwater fishing. However, there are two main differences. The first is that salt water damages equipment, so some tackle is designed to be more resistant to salt damage. The second is that generally, the fish caught in salt water are larger and more aggressive than freshwater fish. As a result, saltwater anglers typically need larger and sturdier tackle.

It is possible for an angler to get a bit wet while fishing from a beach.

Some saltwater rods are very long and strong.

RODS

Some overlap exists in the kinds of fishing rods used for freshwater and saltwater fishing. Spinning rods and casting rods can be used in fresh and salt water. In addition, saltwater anglers can use trolling and jigging rods.

When choosing rods, the main thing to consider is the job the rod will be doing. When fishing from the beach and casting a longer distance into the ocean, a spinning rod made for surf casting is a good choice. This long rod is able handle heavy weights and lures. These rods might range in length from 7 to 15 feet (2.1 to 4.6 m).

Trolling rods are often short casting rods that are very heavy. Trolling is a fishing technique where the fishing line with its lure or bait is pulled through the water. Typically, this is done from a boat moving slowly through the water.

Trolling rods are often mounted to the back of a boat.

Jigging rods are often short, lightweight spinning or casting rods. Jigging rods must be strong to hold up during the continual jerks to the lure. They are also lightweight so the angler doesn't tire as easily from these motions. A jigging rod can also be used like a casting rod.

Because salt water is harsher and more corrosive on the rod and reel, rod materials need to hold up well in salt water. Fiberglass is the most common material used for saltwater rods. It is sturdy and flexible. Graphite is often used for smaller,

Many saltwater jigging rods are made to be used with braided line.

Anglers can choose from a variety of types of saltwater rods.

lighter rods. Graphite allows the angler to feel a fish picking up the bait more easily than a fiberglass rod does. But graphite is not as durable. Some of the newer saltwater rods are made with a combination of fiberglass and graphite. These rods are both lightweight and durable.

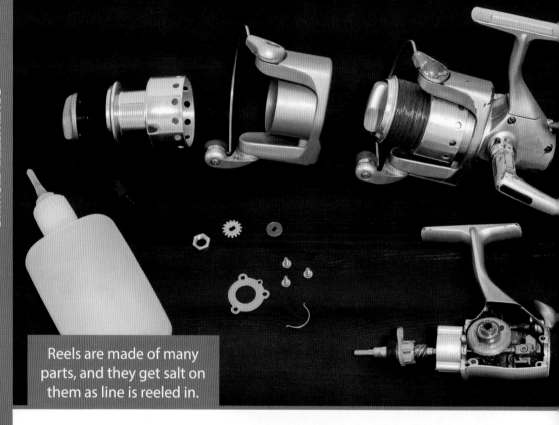

Reels are made of many parts, and they get salt on them as line is reeled in.

No matter which saltwater rod an angler chooses, the angler should always clean the rod well after each fishing trip. The whole rod and reel should be carefully rinsed with fresh water and dried with a towel to get rid of the salt. If salt is left on the rod and reel, it will corrode the metal parts over time.

SPEARFISHING

Not everyone fishes with a rod and reel. In spearfishing, a person throws a spear to catch a fish for eating. It can be done in fresh or salt water. Today, spearfishing is typically done while snorkeling. Some people spearfish with a spear that works something like a simple bow and arrow. Others use a speargun, where the spear is launched from a simple gun device. People who enjoy spearfishing love the up-close view of the underwater world.

REELS

Saltwater reels are similar to freshwater reels. But as with rods, they are made to better withstand the corrosive salt water. Materials like copper and stainless steel are used in saltwater reels because they last longer in the salty environment. A saltwater reel can be used to fish in fresh water. But it would not be wise to use a freshwater reel in salt water.

On boats, reels may have salt water splashed on them as the boat moves.

When fishing from a boat in offshore waters, a heavier bait-casting or spinning reel is a good choice. These large reels are needed to handle the larger fish that can be caught offshore. Anglers who fish inshore waters or on the beach in the surf might use a lighter bait-casting or spinning reel.

Large ocean fish are powerful and need gear strong enough to reel them in.

Although saltwater fishing line needs to be strong, it's also helpful if it's hard for fish to see.

FISHING LINE

The same basic kinds of fishing line are used for freshwater and saltwater fishing. These are monofilament, fluorocarbon, and braided lines. Fishing line comes in bright colors that can be easily seen. However, many saltwater anglers prefer to use clear or camouflaged line so the fish cannot see it. Saltwater fishing line, like freshwater line, is classified based on the line's strength. The pound test of the line describes how many pounds of pressure the line can handle before it breaks. Knowing the general size of the fish an angler might catch helps determine what pound line to use.

Very large fish need big hooks.

HOOKS

The same hook shapes used for freshwater fishing can be used in saltwater fishing as well. It is important to consider the hook's material. High-carbon steel is sturdy, and it rusts. This is important because sometimes when a fish swallows a hook, the angler simply cuts the line and lets the fish swim free. The fish may live without the hook causing it any problems, especially if that hooks rusts away over time. Other saltwater fishing hooks are made from rust-resistant stainless steel. These hooks remain inside fish for a much longer time, possibly causing problems for the fish. For this reason, some anglers avoid using rust-resistant hooks. Or they use a tool called a disgorger, a long rod that reaches deep into a fish to remove the hook.

The choice of a rusting hook is especially important if the angler plans to release the fish.

BAIT

Shrimp is a popular bait for saltwater fishing. Anglers use shrimp—dead or alive, fresh or frozen—to catch fish inshore, in the surf, or on the ocean. Tackle shops sell shrimp bait. However, many anglers catch their own shrimp in inshore waters using a net or a shrimp trap. Flounder, red drums, snapper, cobias, and sea trout are just some of the fish that can be caught with shrimp.

Cut bait is also popular for saltwater fishing. Cut bait includes small fish or squid cut into bite-size pieces. Some anglers fish for small fish that they can cut up to use as bait for larger fish. Bluefish, sea bass, mahi-mahi, sharks, tuna, and cobias are some of the fish that can be caught with cut bait.

Shrimp attract both big and small fish.

Cut bait has a stronger smell than live bait.

Some saltwater fish prefer live bait over cut bait. Live bait includes minnows and other small fish, eels, and shrimp. Shellfish such as clams, mussels, or crabs are another type of live bait for catching saltwater fish. Groupers, snapper, cobias, red drums, tuna, and sharks are some of the fish that can be caught with live bait.

Some ocean fish are caught near the seafloor.

Typically, when anglers are using bait to fish in salt water, they use either a bottom fishing rig or a float rig. The bottom rig is simply a baited hook and a weight attached to the fishing line. The weight takes the bait down to the ocean bottom, where many fish feed. The float rig might be used when fishing from a pier or jetty. With this rig, the float keeps the bait floating in the water at the desired depth where a certain type of fish might be feeding.

DID YOU KNOW?

A person who has a job studying fish is called an ichthyologist. Museums, research laboratories, and colleges are places where an ichthyologist might work.

LURES

Many anglers use the same styles of lures for saltwater fishing as they do for freshwater fishing. Jigs, plugs, soft plastic lures, spinnerbaits, spoons, and surface lures can all work. The one factor to consider is whether the freshwater lure is large and sturdy enough to handle the bigger fish caught in salt water.

Depending on the fish, an angler may need a lure larger than what freshwater fish would require.

OTHER TACKLE

The smaller items of tackle an angler carries are basically the same whether fishing in fresh or salt waters. They include items such as leaders, weights, bobbers, snaps, and swivels. As with other items, larger and sturdier versions might be the best choice. For example, a weight used to fish in the rough ocean surf would need to be quite a bit heavier than the weight used to fish in a quiet pond. A leader used in salt water might need to be longer and heavier than for fresh water because of the bigger fish caught in salt water.

Heavier weights are needed for deeper water, while shallower water requires lighter weights.

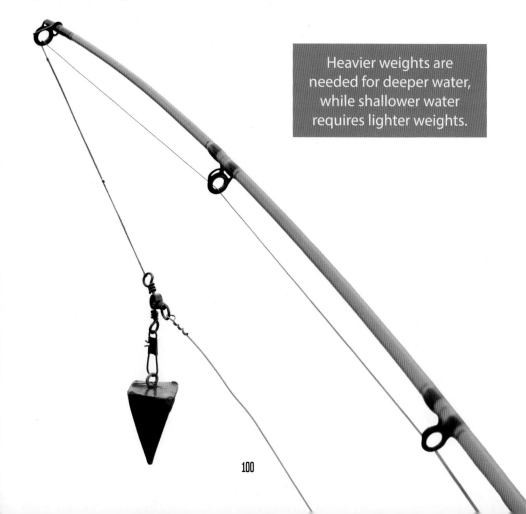

It's important to bring a tackle box that isn't too heavy to carry to and from the fishing spot.

TACKLE BOX

Just like the freshwater tackle box, the saltwater tackle box can be a hard-sided box or a soft-sided bag. A good tackle box can work well for either freshwater or saltwater fishing. Some anglers who fish in both fresh water and salt water prefer to keep two separate tackle boxes to store gear separately.

Saltwater fishing spots are sometimes hard for anglers to get to, but they offer exciting fishing experiences.

WHERE TO GO SALTWATER FISHING

Freshwater anglers can find places to fish nearby almost anywhere in the United States. For saltwater anglers, the choices are not so simple. An angler has to get to coastal waters. But the excitement of saltwater fishing can be well worth the trip. Many anglers are interested in going out on big boats for deep-sea fishing. However, there are a variety of options.

Deep-sea fishing requires going offshore to deep ocean waters to fish. Typically, this kind of fishing is most fun for intermediate or advanced anglers. It usually involves paying a boat captain for a half-day or full-day fishing trip. The kinds of large fish that can be caught on these fishing trips include tuna, dolphinfish, wahoos, and marlins.

Although deep-sea fishing offers large and exciting catches, there is no guarantee an angler will catch anything.

Bays and estuaries can be great places for saltwater fishing. The Chesapeake Bay on the Atlantic coast and the San Francisco Bay on the Pacific coast are just two examples of bays with good saltwater fishing. An estuary is where a river flows into the ocean. In estuaries, anglers

People may take small fishing boats to deeper bay waters.

Kayaks allow anglers to access shallower bodies of saltwater such as bays.

can catch freshwater and saltwater fish. A variety of fish swim between fresh water and salt water when it is time for mating and laying their eggs. Tarpon, striped bass, shad, salmon, and sea trout are caught in bays and estuaries.

A little bit inshore from the ocean are the flats. Flats are shallow saltwater areas. They are also called backwaters. Most anglers use small boats or kayaks for flats fishing. Red drums, sea trout, and flounder are just a few of the fish that anglers catch while fishing the flats.

Fishing piers can be busy.

Pier fishing is another way for anglers to catch saltwater fish. There is often a charge to fish from a public pier. These passes can be purchased at the pier house before walking out onto the pier. The pier house is a good place to ask questions about what fish are biting and what lures or bait might be good to use. Sea trout, bluefish, flounder, and striped bass are some of the fish caught from piers. Anglers should be very aware of their surroundings when pier fishing. On a busy fishing day, many people might be casting their lines at the same time. It is important for anglers to pay attention to others so no one gets accidentally hooked.

With surf fishing, anglers stand on the beach or wade out into the water and cast the line over the waves. Anglers fishing in the surf might use anywhere from a 7-foot (2.1 m) rod to catch smaller fish to a 15-foot (4.6 m) rod when fishing for striped bass or sharks. They might use extra weights because the current is strong near the beach. Pier fishing and surf fishing are both great ways for beginners to try saltwater fishing.

Surf fishing offers the ability to move along the shoreline and even wade into the water to find just the right spot to catch fish.

HOW TO CATCH SALTWATER FISH

Many of the techniques a beginning saltwater angler needs to learn are the same techniques used to catch freshwater fish. One factor to keep in mind when planning a saltwater fishing trip is the tides. The rising

A fishing spot will experience both high tide and low tide twice a day.

DATE

SEA-LEVEL (METRES)

2.4 m
2 m
1.6 m
1.2 m
0.8 m
0.4 m
0 m
-0.4 m

TIME

00 02 04 06 08 10 12 14 16 18 20 22

LOW TIDE   HIGH TIDE

People of all ages can enjoy saltwater fishing.

and falling of the tides affect saltwater fishing, as fish move and feed based on the tides. Local tackle shops or the pier house can provide tide charts. They can also answer questions about where the fish might be at what time based on the tides.

SALTWATER FISH SPECIES

There are many kinds of saltwater fish anglers like to catch. Each species requires a slightly different approach. Anglers can best plan a fishing excursion when they know which species they want to catch.

Saltwater fish can grow very large and put up good fights.

The Atlantic croaker makes a croaking sound by vibrating its swim bladder.

ATLANTIC CROAKERS

The Atlantic croaker lives along the Atlantic coast and in the Gulf of Mexico. It is one of the most plentiful fish found along North America's Atlantic coast. Croakers get their name from the croaking sound they make. Adult croakers are silver in color and have three to five pairs of tiny barbels on their chins. These fish grow to be about 1 foot (0.3 m) long and weigh up to 2 pounds (0.9 kg). Croakers can be caught in the summer and fall months. Dead shrimp is a good bait for hooking a croaker.

Smaller black sea bass
are a dark brown.

BLACK SEA BASS

Black sea bass live along the Atlantic coast from Maine to
Florida. They migrate away from the coast and head south for
the winter months. These fish return to waters in the north and
to inshore coastal waters for the spring and summer months.
They spawn in the coastal waters, mainly between Long Island
in New York and the Chesapeake Bay near Maryland and
Virginia. After black sea bass spawn, the larger females reverse
sex and become males.

These fish are also called sea bass, blackfish, rock bass, black bass, and tallywag. Black sea bass typically grow to be about 1 foot (0.3 m) long, but some can be up to 2 feet (0.6 m) long. These fish have a bluish-black color. Their color is more brilliant blue while the fish are in the water. Out of the water, their coloring is black and white. These fish swim near structures such as pilings, jetties, rocky areas, buoys, or wrecks. So casting a line near structures in the water can be a good way to catch one of these fish.

Black sea bass eat many types of prey.

BLUE MARLINS

The blue marlin is one of the biggest fish on Earth. It grows to be 14 feet (4.3 m) long and can weigh almost 2,000 pounds (907 kg). Anglers catch blue marlins offshore along the Atlantic and Pacific coasts, in the Gulf

DID YOU KNOW?

There are about 32,000 fish species in the world. There are more fish species than all the other vertebrate species (mammals, birds, reptiles, and amphibians) combined.

The blue marlin typically spends its time near the surface of deep ocean waters.

Many people enjoy the meat of a blue marlin.

of Mexico, and in the waters around Hawaii. The blue marlin is blue with silver-white coloring along its belly. It is easily recognized by its spear-shaped upper jaw, which is called its bill. The marlin uses this bill to attack its prey. For many anglers, landing a blue marlin is the catch of a lifetime.

Bluefish put up a good fight when hooked.

BLUEFISH

Bluefish live along the Atlantic coast from Maine down to eastern Florida. They migrate south to warmer waters in the winter and back to northern waters during the summer. These fish have blue-green backs with silver coloring on the bellies and sides. The fish can grow to be nearly 4 feet (1.2 m) long and up to 30 pounds (14 kg). Bluefish have powerful jaws and razor-sharp teeth. Anglers who catch bluefish keep their fingers away from the fish's mouth to avoid getting bitten.

When schools of large bluefish find schools of small baitfish swimming near the water's surface, the bluefish feed in a frenzy called the "bluefish blitz." During these feedings, the

seawater churns and swirls like water in a washing machine. Anglers looks for these churning waters and cast their lines where the fish are busily feeding.

A bluefish's teeth are shaped like cones.

BONEFISH

Bonefish live in coastal tropical waters, such as creeks, rivers, and bays. Hawaii and the coasts of south Florida and California are places where anglers catch bonefish. Other names for the

Bonefish have dark stripes that run the length of their bodies.

Bonefish feed in shallow water.

bonefish include banana fish and ladyfish. These fish are silver with darker streaks along their sides. The fish's snout is an unusual cone shape. Anglers have nicknamed bonefish the "gray ghost" because the fish are fast and hard to find. Bonefish can be more than 2.5 feet (0.8 m) long and weigh about 14 pounds (6.4 kg). Bonefish are powerful and fast. They are a favorite of many anglers because they put up a strong fight. Bonefish feed on shrimp and crabs, so anglers often use these as bait.

Another name for the dolphinfish is the dorado.

DOLPHINFISH

Dolphinfish are also called mahi-mahi, especially when they are eaten. Dolphinfish are not dolphins. These fish live in tropical waters, such as those near Hawaii, the Gulf of Mexico, and the Atlantic and Pacific coasts. Dolphinfish are colorful with metallic blue and green coloring on their sides. Their bellies are white and yellow. These fish can grow to be 6 feet (1.8 m) long. But it is more typical for anglers to catch dolphinfish that are about 3 feet (0.9 m) long. People enjoy eating dolphinfish, and they are a prized catch for anglers.

Dolphinfish are fast swimmers.

FLATFISH

Flatfish is the name for a number of fish with thin, flat bodies. The distinctive feature of the flatfish is that both its eyes are on one side of its body. These fish lie flat on the seafloor with both eyes looking up. Their colors change to match their surroundings, letting them hide from predators.

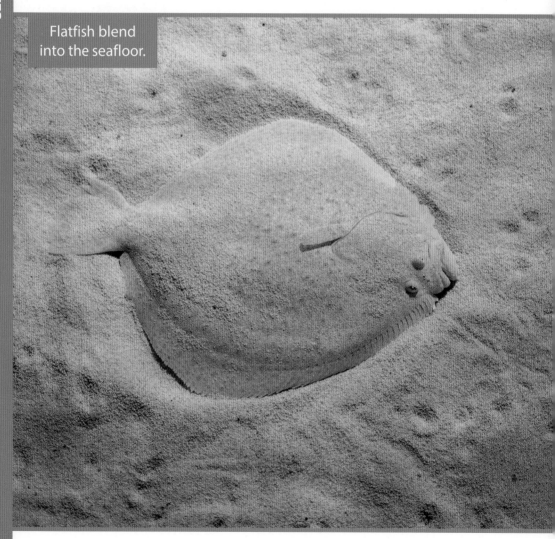

Flatfish blend into the seafloor.

Flatfish is eaten in many ways, including raw as sashimi.

Flounder and halibut are two types of flatfish caught in the United States. Some species can grow up to 15 feet (4.6 m) long. When flatfish hatch, they have an eye on each side of their heads. As they grow, one eye begins to move, and their bodies become flat. After that change, flatfish spend most of their time settled on the ocean bottom. Anglers fish for flatfish using bait or lures. For lures, many anglers choose small jigs or bucktails. Favorite bait for catching flatfish includes minnows, squid, finger mullets, or shrimp.

DID YOU KNOW?

The best time to fish in Alaska is the summer and fall. Anglers say the best freshwater fishing happens in May through September. For saltwater fishing, the best time is the spring months through November.

Some lingcod live near California's Channel Islands.

LINGCOD

Lingcod live along the Pacific coast and in the waters near Alaska. This fish has the nickname "buckethead" because of the large size of its head and mouth. Its body is long and narrow. The fish is dark gray and brown with copper spots on its back. Its coloring gives it a camouflaged appearance. Lingcod can grow to be 5 feet (1.5 m) long and weigh 80 pounds (36 kg). They are popular for eating.

RED DRUMS

The red drum is also called the redfish or channel bass. When the fish is one to four years old, it is called a puppy drum. Red drums live in the ocean and in rivers and bays near the coast from New England to Florida and along the Gulf coast. Red drums typically grow to be about 2.5 feet (0.8 m) long. But some can be 5 feet (1.5 m) long and weigh as much as 90 pounds (41 kg).

The red drum is caught for fun and is also caught and sold for food.

These fish are a reddish-bronze color. The males make a croaking or drum-like noise during spawning season by vibrating a muscle in their bodies. Red drums are related to other fish like the black drum, spotted sea trout, Atlantic croakers, and spot. These other fish also make the croaking or drum sound. The red drum has a large spot that looks like an eye near its tail. Scientists believe that this spot tricks predators into attacking the tail instead of the head. This allows time for the fish to escape its predator. Many anglers fish for red drum at night. The best bait includes soft-shell crabs, clams, shrimp, and spot.

Most red drums have at least one spot per side, but some have two or more on a side.

SPOT

Spot live in the ocean, in rivers, and in bays along the Atlantic coast and the Gulf of Mexico. They are sometimes called the Norfolk spot. These fish have blue-gray coloring on their backs with yellow or yellow-white bellies. Their fins are pale yellow. The spot gets its name from the large, black spot just above its gills. These fish have wavy horizontal stripes along their bodies. Spot can grow to be about 1 foot (0.3 m) long. Spot rarely weigh more than 1 pound (0.5 kg). Typically, anglers catch spot that are 6 to 8 inches (15 to 20 cm) long.

The spot's scientific name is *Leiostomus xanthurus*.

Spot live in sandy, shallow waters during the summer months. When cooler weather arrives, they move offshore to live in deeper waters. They are one of the most abundant fish in the coastal waters of the southeastern United States. Anglers fish for spot in the surf or from piers, jetties, or bridges. Shrimp, squid, or bloodworms make good bait. Spot live in schools, so where anglers catch one, there are usually plenty more to be found.

SPOTTED SEA TROUT

The spotted sea trout is found in the ocean, rivers, and bays near the coast from New England to southern Florida and

along the Gulf coast. The spotted sea trout is also called the speckled trout or weakfish. This fish's name is deceptive because it is not actually a trout. Actual trout belong to the same fish family as salmon. The spotted sea trout belongs to the same fish family as redfish, black drums, and Atlantic croakers. The spotted sea trout is silvery with dark spots along its body. It can grow to be more than 3 feet (0.9 m) long. Shrimp is good bait for catching these fish. Artificial lures such as soft plastic shrimp, plastic tail grub jigs, and spoons can also be effective.

Spotted sea trout eat fish and crustaceans such as shrimp.

SHARKS

Anglers fish for sharks on both the Atlantic and Pacific coasts. Sharks that are commonly fished include some types of mako, threshers, blacktip, sandbar, and tiger sharks that aren't endangered. Anglers typically use cut bait to catch sharks. Sharks can be caught in the surf, from public piers,

Mako sharks will often leap out of the water when hooked.

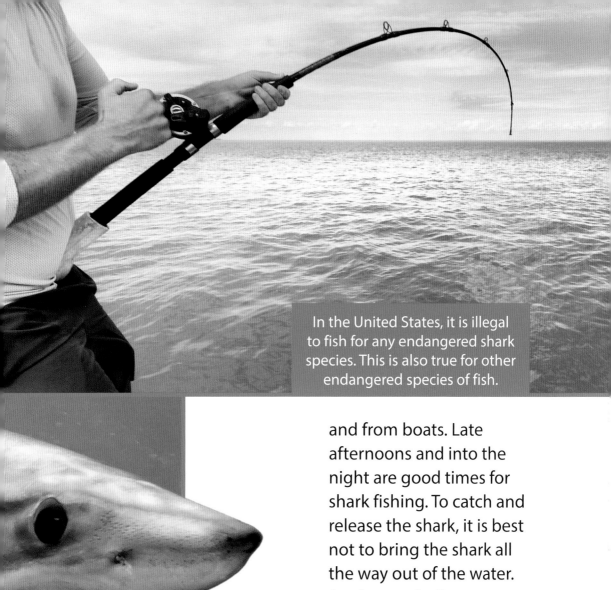

In the United States, it is illegal to fish for any endangered shark species. This is also true for other endangered species of fish.

and from boats. Late afternoons and into the night are good times for shark fishing. To catch and release the shark, it is best not to bring the shark all the way out of the water. Anglers typically use long-handle pliers or a long hook remover to get the hook out of the shark's mouth. If the shark has swallowed the hook, a pair of bolt cutters can be used to cut the wire leader.

Adult swordfish don't have scales.

SWORDFISH

Swordfish can weigh more than 1,000 pounds (450 kg). However, most of the swordfish caught weigh between 50 and 200 pounds (23 and 91 kg). They are black or brown on their backs, with the coloring fading on their bellies. The swordfish has a long, pointed upper jaw, which is shaped like a

GOOD EATING!

Many of the fish that anglers catch taste good and are healthy meal choices. The American Heart Association recommends that people eat fish at least twice a week because they are good for heart and brain health. Healthy fish include Alaska salmon, cod, herring, mahi-mahi, mackerel, perch, rainbow trout, sardines, striped bass, and skipjack tuna. Some fish should not be eaten because they could contain high levels of mercury or other contaminants. A few of the fish to avoid are sharks, swordfish, king mackerel, and tilefish.

sword or spear. Like marlins, swordfish use their sharp bills to attack and slash prey. Quick and powerful, swordfish can swim up to 50 miles per hour (80 kmh). Anglers catch swordfish offshore along the Atlantic and Pacific coasts, in the Gulf of Mexico, and in the waters around Hawaii.

Swordfish are listed as near threatened by the International Union for Conservation of Nature (IUCN).

TUNA

Tuna are powerful fish found in the world's oceans. In the United States, anglers catch tuna offshore of the Atlantic and Pacific coasts and in the waters around Hawaii. Most tuna are apex predators, meaning that as adults, no other animal hunts them. Tuna are good to eat, so anglers catch them for a tasty meal. But anglers also

The yellowfin tuna typically stays near the ocean's surface.

Bluefin tuna are closely regulated by the US government to keep the populations at healthy numbers.

enjoy the thrill of catching these powerful game fish. There are several species of tuna. The smallest is the bullet tuna, which weighs about 4 pounds (1.8 kg). The largest is the Atlantic bluefin tuna, which has an average weight around 500 pounds (227 kg). Some tuna can swim as fast as 43 miles per hour (69 kmh).

FLY-FISHING

Fly-fishing is often done in streams.

Fly-fishing is a type of fishing that can be done in either fresh water or salt water. Some anglers find fly-fishing more challenging than other types of freshwater and saltwater fishing. In fly-fishing, the angler uses specialized gear, a special casting technique, and artificial flies to attract the fish. The angler tries to make it look like an insect has landed on the surface of the water. Once an angler learns the casting technique, fly-fishing provides yet another exciting way to catch fish. In 2019 about seven million people in the United States went fly-fishing.

RODS AND LINES

Fly rods and fly lines are sized based on a number scale from one to 14, from lightest to heaviest. Anglers generally match the number of the line to the number of the rod. So they would use number five line with a number five rod. A rod will typically have a number printed on it suggesting what weight of fly line works well on that rod.

Fly rods tend to be a bit lighter than other fishing rods.

The number one line and rod are slender and delicate, while the number 14 line and rod are sturdy and heavy. When fishing for smaller fish, like panfish or small trout, an angler might use fly line and rod weights numbers one, two, or three. For larger panfish or larger trout, a fly line and rod weight number four can be used. Line and rod weights numbers five and six are good weights for

Fly line is often heavy and brightly colored.

Long casts can be especially helpful in wide-open areas.

trout and bass fishing. Fly line and rod weight number seven is used when fishing for larger fish, such as steelhead trout, bass, and smaller salmon. The fly line and rod weights eight and higher are typically used for large, powerful fish, such as larger freshwater salmon and saltwater fish. Generally, anglers can make longer casts with the heavier fly lines. Fly line and rod weights numbers four, five, and six are good weights for anglers just learning to fly-fish.

Small fish may not require backing, but it's often good to have backing for larger fish.

In addition to the fly line, fly-fishers use backing, which is a strong section of line that attaches the fly line to the reel. Generally, fly line is 100 feet (30 m) long. If a fish grabs the angler's hook and starts swimming away for a long distance, it might reach the end of the 100 feet (30 m) of fly line. The backing gives the angler extra yards of strong line. If an angler hooks a large,

TENKARA RODS

A tenkara rod is a special type of fly-fishing rod invented for fishing the mountain streams in Japan. These rods have gained popularity with anglers around the world. The lightweight rods are telescoping, meaning they collapse down to a small size and expand for fishing. This makes them easy to pack and carry. This simple rod has no reel. The angler's hands and the rod are used to control the line. A tenkara rod can be used to catch smaller fish, like small trout and panfish.

fast fish, the added backing gives the angler extra line to fight the fish. The fish will tire itself out more before the angler reels it in. In addition, backing makes the reel fuller. This means that when turning the handle to reel in line, more line will be brought in with one crank than it would if the reel were almost empty. This helps the angler fight and land the fish more efficiently.

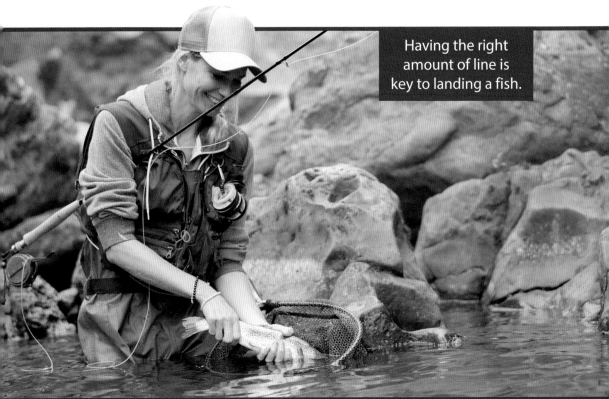

Having the right amount of line is key to landing a fish.

REELS

Fly-fishing reels come in different sizes and shapes. Reels can be made of aluminum, carbon fiber, stainless steel, or magnesium. Aluminum reels tend to be less expensive. These reels require good care and cleaning to prevent corrosion over time. Reels made from titanium or carbon fiber typically cost more but last longer.

The most important job of the fly reel is to hold line. Anglers may not even use it to reel in a fish, choosing instead to pull in the line with their hands.

Fly fishers have loose line pulled out from the reel when fishing, which they control with their hand to reel in line between casts.

Anglers usually choose their reels depending on the kind of fly-fishing they plan to do. The number sizes on the reel closely align to the fly line and rod number sizes. Most fly-fishing reels are numbered 3/4 weight, 5 weight, 6/7 weight, 8/9 weight, and 10/12 weight. Anglers usually put together their fly-fishing tackle with the rod, line, and reel all having similar weight numbers.

It takes skill to make a fly.

FLIES

In regular freshwater or saltwater fishing, anglers use bait or artificial lures to catch fish. In fly-fishing, the angler uses artificial flies to catch the fish. Fly-fishing flies are lures designed to look like creatures that a fish might want to eat—tiny insects, baitfish, worms, leeches, or frogs. They can be created to look like either the immature or adult stages of these creatures. Flies are tied by hand using materials such as feathers, fur, wool, thread, and hair, along with a hook. Fly tying requires special skill and equipment. It is also based on observation. People who tie flies have a strong knowledge of the creatures they are trying to imitate, how they move in and around the water, and when they hatch and rise out of the water. Anglers have many options when it comes to choosing flies, but most fishing flies fall into four broad categories.

Anglers keep several flies on hand, selecting the type based on what they're fishing.

Dry fly

Dry flies imitate insects that land on the water's surface. These can resemble mayflies, stoneflies, caddis flies, grasshoppers, midges, dragonflies, beetles, or water bugs. Dry flies are very lightweight and made to sit on the water's surface like the creatures they imitate. Anglers use dry flies when fly-fishing on rivers and lakes. They catch panfish, bass, and trout with these flies.

Nymphs are flies that look like young waterborne insects in larval form. These flies might resemble mayflies, stoneflies, or caddis flies in their larval stage, moving near the bottom of the water. The nymphs are made with a tiny weight attached so they can be fished below the water's surface. Anglers fish these flies near the bottoms of rivers and lakes, allowing the flies to bump along on the rocky bottom. They catch panfish, trout, steelhead trout, and salmon with nymphs.

Nymph fly

Streamers are flies that look like small baitfish, crayfish, or leeches. They are also made to look like very young trout, perch, or bass. Anglers move streamers through the water to look like a baitfish darting around, hoping to attract the attention of a larger fish.

Streamer fly

Top-water flies are another type of fly. While they are fished on the surface of the water, they are different from dry flies. The top-water flies are made to look like frogs, cicadas, small mice, and even little birds. Fly tiers make these flies using balsa wood, foam, or spun deer hair. The hook is part of the fly. So unless anglers are tying their own flies, they do not need to buy hooks separately.

Top-water fly

An angler pinches a split shot weight onto fishing line.

TACKLE

In regular freshwater or saltwater fishing, the weights are tied at the end of the fishing line to help the bait or lure sink down into the water. Fly-fishing weights serve the same purpose of helping the fly sink into the water, but they are made differently. Fly-fishing weights are small round or egg-shaped balls, roughly the size of a pea with a slit in the middle. They are called split shots. With the slit in the middle of the split shot, the angler can easily secure the weight by pinching it onto the line. Once it is pinched, it does not slide or move. The split shots are made of lead or tin.

The leader, often about 9 feet (2.7 m) long, is the clear line that attaches on the end of the fly line. The leader is typically heavier line that tapers to be thinner where it connects to the tippet. The tippet is a lighter-weight piece of line that connects the leader to the fly.

The tippet needs to be strong but lightweight so it is not easily noticed by the fish. The tippet is not essential in fly-fishing. But many anglers consider it an important piece of tackle because it allows them to control the line and fly in ways that imitate the movements of the actual insects. The tippet also adds length to the angler's line. This added length is helpful when fishing in wide streams and rivers or ocean waters. The leader and tippet are typically made of monofilament or fluorocarbon. The monofilament is a less expensive choice. It floats easily on the water. The fluorocarbon is more expensive. Fish have a hard time seeing the almost invisible fluorocarbon. It sinks faster than monofilament and is more durable.

The tippet is very thin where it connects with the fly.

TACKLE BOX AND FLY BOX

A regular tackle box or tackle bag is helpful for carrying the gear used in fly-fishing. Most anglers who fly-fish also have a fly box. These boxes are specially designed to organize and carry the many small flies an angler uses. Fly boxes come in a variety of sizes.

Fly boxes help keep flies secure but easy to access.

This angler is fly-fishing in the Caribbean Sea.

WHERE TO GO FLY-FISHING

Photographs often show anglers fly-fishing in rivers running through mountain scenery. Those mountain rivers and streams are great places for fly-fishing. But an angler does not have to travel to the mountains to fish. Plenty of other places are suitable for fly-fishing.

Shallow rivers and streams are common fly-fishing spots.

Rivers and streams where the water stays cold year-round are great places to fly-fish for trout. In these types of waters, trout tend to hide in deep pools of water and along the shore where logs, bushes, or large rocks give them hiding places. An angler might also catch small bass in these cold-water rivers. Trout can also be caught in ponds and lakes where the water is always cold. Ideal times to fish in these waters are just after sunrise and just before dark. Fish are often active feeders at these times, so they are more likely to chase a fly on a line.

Trout eat insects, so fly-fishing is a good way to catch them.

Ponds, lakes, and rivers where waters are warmer are great places to fly-fish for panfish like bluegills and other sunfish or crappies. These fish like to hide in weedy areas and around structures like boat docks. During the summer months, as the waters warm, the larger bluegills head toward

SALTWATER FLY-FISHING

Fly-fishing is more commonly done in fresh water. But fly-fishing also happens in salt water. Anglers fly-fish in inshore salt waters, such as bays, channels, and estuaries. Fish in these waters usually move with the tides and are looking for small baitfish to eat. Tarpon, barracuda, bonefish, striped bass, and redfish are just some of the saltwater fish anglers catch when fly-fishing.

The shallow parts of lakes can make good fly-fishing locations.

Smallmouth bass will bite flies.

deeper waters. To reach the fish there, anglers sometimes fish from a canoe or kayak. Bass and pickerel can sometimes be caught fly-fishing in warmer waters. The bass and pickerel hide under lily pads, in weedy areas, and near boat docks.

A fly-fishing cast sends line out ahead of the fly.

HOW TO FLY-FISH

Learning to cast is the challenging first step of learning to be a fly-fishing angler. The cast in fly-fishing is different from casting a rod with regular freshwater or saltwater gear. In regular fishing, the angler casts the lure or bait, and the line follows the lure or bait. With fly-fishing, the angler casts the line. Because the fly is so light, the fly then follows the line. Some anglers compare casting to hammering a nail into the wall, with the rod grip being like the hammer handle. Casting is a short stroke, like hammering, that stops suddenly. Many videos online show beginners how to cast.

The overhead cast is a basic cast in fly-fishing. Once anglers master the overhead cast, they can learn other fly casts like the roll cast, two-stroke cast, haul cast, or wind cast. Learning to cast a fly rod can be practiced at home before going to the water to fish. A beginner can ask an experienced angler friend to demonstrate the casting techniques. Also, some fly tackle shops offer fly casting lessons.

People can practice casting on land.

Staying safe while fishing is important. The proper clothing and footwear can help. Fishing can be messy, so most anglers choose clothes they do not mind getting dirty. Depending on the outdoor temperatures, dressing in layers can be smart. As the temperature rises during the day, an angler can peel off the outer layers. There are shirts designed specifically for fishing. They are typically made of nylon,

When fishing in winter, it's especially important to wear warm clothes.

Tan and green blend in with dirt, trees, and grasses along the shore.

so they dry quickly when they get wet. Some fishing shirts are treated to give added protection against the sun. Fishing shirts usually have a few vent holes around the body to allow for good air circulation. This helps keep anglers from getting too hot in warmer weather.

Some anglers fish in shallow waters, where fish are close to the surface and can see the angler. In these situations, the angler might choose clothing in colors such as gray, brown, and dark green to blend in with the surroundings.

Some people wear waterproof boots to keep their feet dry.

Many anglers prefer pants made of nylon. Nylon is lightweight, dries quickly, and is easier to move around in than cotton, especially if it gets wet. Some anglers choose pants with plenty of pockets because it allows them to keep small tools they need for fishing in an easy-to-reach place.

For shoes, anglers choose sandals, water shoes, sneakers, or boots. The key is to be sure the shoes have nonslip treads and are made of waterproof or quick-dry materials. Closed-toe sandals, like hiking sandals, also work well.

Fishing gloves are helpful for several reasons. When removing a fish from the hook, the gloves protect the angler's hands from being cut or scratched by the sharp points on the fish's fins. The gloves also allow the angler to get a better grip on the slippery fish's body. The gloves make it easier for the angler to safely handle the fish without hurting it.

Fishing gloves can protect both the angler and the fish.

Hats and sunglasses are also smart choices for anglers, who may be standing out in the sun for long hours. Hats protect anglers from heat and sunburn. Even when wearing a long-sleeve shirt or a hat, it is also wise to keep sunscreen handy and apply it generously. Sunglasses help an angler see when there is sun glare on the water. They can also protect the eyes from being hooked.

Hats that shade both the face and the back of the neck are best for long hours in the sun.

Fishing vests and waders are both helpful in fly-fishing, where people typically stand in shallow water away from their tackle boxes.

Some anglers like to wear fishing vests. These are especially popular for fly-fishing. The vests have pockets and clips that are handy for carrying small tackle and tools. For anglers who fish by walking into the water to cast their lines, waders can be an important purchase. Waders keep the angler dry up to the waist or chest while fishing. They are usually made from waterproof materials like PVC, neoprene, or nylon.

DID YOU KNOW?

About 70 percent of Earth is covered in water. Most of Earth's water is found in the ocean— about 96 percent of Earth's water is salt water.

In addition to wearing life jackets, anglers should be prepared for many different types of weather when going out in a boat.

LIFE JACKETS

When fishing from a boat, a life jacket is an essential piece of safety gear. Many states have laws requiring children to wear life jackets on moving boats. In states with no life jacket laws in place, the US Coast Guard requires children younger than age 13 to wear a life jacket.

TACKLE BOX SAFETY

The tackle box is full of sharp objects that could cut or injure an angler. With a little caution, anglers can prevent many fishing accidents. Anglers should keep sharp objects like knives, pliers, scissors, or hooks inside the tackle box when they are not being used. Knives or hooks lying around on the ground could easily be stepped on. If a group of people are fishing together, each angler should take time to see where others are standing before casting a line. This can prevent accidentally hooking someone.

Anglers can keep their tackle boxes closed when not in use to keep sharp objects secure.

When removing a hook from a fish's mouth, it helps to stay calm, even though catching a fish can be exciting. Wearing fishing gloves and using pliers can also protect anglers' hands when removing the hook.

WATCH THE WEATHER

Because fishing is always an outdoor activity, anglers must watch the weather. Knowing the

Forceps are another tool that can help anglers safely remove hooks from the mouths of fish.

It's safest to fish from a boat when the water is calm.

temperature forecast helps anglers know how to dress for a day of fishing. Being aware of approaching thunderstorms is important. For anglers on a boat, thunderstorms can bring wind, waves, lightning, and rain. These conditions can quickly put boaters in serious danger. Lightning is also a danger for anglers on land. The National Weather Service recommends that boaters not head out if there is a chance of thunderstorms. Anglers who do get caught out in a thunderstorm should move to port or a safe shelter as quickly as possible.

Some stores, such as tackle shops, sell fishing licenses.

Most states require a fishing license, even if the angler is just catching and releasing the fish. The US Fish and Wildlife Service website lists information about fishing licenses needed for every state, including freshwater and saltwater licenses. Licenses can usually be purchased for a single day or for a year of fishing. Some states offer a lifetime license that does not need to be renewed each year. Licenses can be purchased online, by phone, or at the county tax collector's office. Some states do not require licenses for young children or senior adults.

Some states, including Maine, have days when people can fish for free without a license.

Fishing License Required
For Ages 16 And Up
FGC 7145
O.C.C.O. 2-5-63(d)
All Fish and Wildlife Codes Enforced

Some places post reminders about the need for a fishing license, but it is the angler's responsibility to get a license no matter the fishing spot.

Usually if an angler is fishing at a pond on private property, a license is not needed. But permission is needed from the person who owns the property. Licensing also varies from state to state. For example, one state might require a license for a person fishing from a public pier, while another state does not. Some states have specific rules about the kind of equipment an angler can use. Every angler should become familiar with the rules and the licenses needed in the state where he or she is fishing.

INVASIVE SPECIES

An invasive species is a plant or animal introduced into waters that are not native for that species. An invasive fish species can harm native plants and animals. These fish may reproduce quickly and have few predators to reduce their numbers. The large invasive population may then eat most of the food a native species eats. For example, carp from Asia were brought to the United States to stock small ponds. They have accidentally gotten into the Mississippi River, where they are eating plants in native fish spawning grounds. Anglers can help protect the waters against invasive species. One way to do this is to dump any unwanted bait, such as worms or fish parts, into a trash can instead of in the water. Another step is to clean the boat and fishing gear well before moving from one body of water to another. If anglers see invasive species in the water, they can report it to the state's department of natural resources or fish and wildlife office.

Wildlife officers can ask to see a person's fishing license and issue a ticket if the angler doesn't have it on hand.

FISH LIMITS AND REGULATIONS

To protect fish populations, there are laws that regulate recreational fishing. The National Oceanic and Atmospheric Administration (NOAA) is the federal government agency that sets the laws for fishing in the United States.

These laws set limits on certain fish species that need protection. For example, the law might state that an angler can catch only a certain number of a particular type of fish. Or the law might state that only fish of a certain size can be caught. The law might allow a fish to be caught only at certain times of the year. If anglers catch a fish that cannot be legally caught, such as one that is too small or caught out of season,

NOAA studies fish populations to set guidelines.

NOAA researchers can find a fish's age by studying its ears. Knowing the age of fish in an area helps scientists determine if the population is healthy.

they must release it back to the water as quickly and safely as possible. By protecting the fish when they are small or during the spawning season, the laws work to ensure that anglers today and in future generations can enjoy recreational fishing.

Both commercial and recreational fishing can contribute to overfishing.

Some fish are at risk due to overfishing. Overfishing occurs when fish are taken from a body of water faster than they can reproduce. The fish population gradually declines. Both commercial fishing vessels and recreational anglers can contribute to the problem of overfishing. Licenses and catch limits help prevent overfishing.

Another problem that can occur alongside overfishing is bycatch. This happens in commercial fishing when sea life such as turtles, whales, porpoises, or dolphins get caught in nets along with the fish. These sea creatures die as an unintended consequence of the commercial fishing. NOAA Fisheries, a part of the US federal government, works to reduce bycatch. It ensures commercial anglers understand bycatch and are fishing in ways that minimize it.

When fishing with nets, several other species can be caught as bycatch along with the target species.

It is important for anglers to be familiar with the regulations. Ignorance of the fishing regulations is not an excuse. Catching and keeping a fish illegally can result in a fine. The state fish and wildlife agency enforces the fishing rules. Typically this agency has information online about fishing rules and limits.

Fish hatcheries are places where people raise fish to stock bodies of water.

Fish are often moved into a body of water through a tube that runs from a tank into the water.

FISH STOCKING

Fish stocking is the practice of adding fish to bodies of water. Sometimes a state will add a large number of young fish to a river, reservoir, or lake so that anglers will have more fish to catch. Sometimes fish are stocked to manage the other fish species in the waters. For example, if one species of fish is reproducing quickly and taking over the body of water, predator fish might be added to the water to balance out the population of the fish that are too abundant. Most of the time, fish stocking is done by a state's wildlife agency. But sometimes people will stock their own private ponds as well.

Anglers can avoid lifting a fish out of the water if they plan to release it.

CATCH AND RELEASE

For recreational anglers, one way to help the overfishing problem is to practice catch and release fishing. A fish that is caught and released might still die because of the stress and injury to its body while it is pulled from the water and handled. Anglers can help keep the fish healthier by using a net to lift the fish out of the water. If anglers keep their hands wet or wear fishing gloves when handling the fish, they avoid disturbing the protective mucus that covers the fish's body to prevent infection.

Anglers should
handle fish only as
much as is necessary.

Once a fish is lifted out of the water, anglers should move quickly to remove the hook and get the fish back into the water. If the fish has swallowed the hook deeply, the safest thing is often to cut the line and

Anglers can even try to remove the hook while the fish is in the water.

Releasing a fish gives it the chance to continue to grow and reproduce, ensuring there will be fish to catch in the future.

leave the hook in the fish. Gently holding the fish, the angler places the fish back in the water and watches to see if the gills are opening and closing. Then the fish can swim to safety.

DO FISH FEEL PAIN?

For generations, people have believed that fish do not feel pain. However, more and more studies suggest that fish can feel pain, just not in the same ways that humans do. Laws exist to protect animals like chickens, cows, dogs, and cats from inhumane treatment. But no laws protect fish. As the scientific understanding of how fish experience pain grows, some people have begun to advocate for laws that protect fish in the same ways.

Trash can harm wildlife.

TAKING CARE OF THE WATERWAYS

Fresh and salt waters are a resource that all humans share. For those waters and the creatures that live in them to remain healthy for generations to come, the waters must be protected. Because anglers are near the waters regularly, they play an important role in keeping the waters healthy and the fish populations strong. Anglers should never leave litter behind when fishing. Many anglers carry a bag for gathering litter until they can place it in a trash or recycling can. Anglers can also collect and dispose of any litter they find that others have left behind.

Picking up trash will make fishing spots more enjoyable for everyone.

Some anglers choose to swap a treble hook for a single hook when fishing. A single hook does less damage to the fish when an angler is planning to catch and release. Some anglers pinch down the barb of the hook or fish with barbless hooks, because these do less damage to the fish. The barb is the pointy piece just below the sharp tip of the hook that points in the opposite direction of the hook.

A single hook can go through only one spot on the fish, but a treble hook can go through several.

Anglers enjoy searching for their next big fish.

It helps ensure that the hook stays in place in the fish's mouth by preventing it from slipping backward.

Whether it is labeled a hobby or a sport, fishing is an activity that people can enjoy for a lifetime. Freshwater fishing is easily accessible across the United States. For people who live near the coasts or can travel there, saltwater fishing is an exciting option. People of all ages have discovered fishing as a good way to spend time in nature, have fun, and even catch their own food.

DID YOU KNOW?

An angler cannot know whether water is polluted just by looking at it. Some fish caught in polluted waters might be harmful if eaten. If anglers want to eat the fish they catch, the US Environmental Protection Agency recommends contacting the local or state environmental health department before fishing to see if any advisories are posted for the fish in that area.

GLOSSARY

anadromous
Relating to a fish that migrates between fresh water and salt water.

artificial
Made by humans; not natural.

bay
An inlet set off from a main body of water.

cast
To throw the bait or lure into the water using a fishing rod.

catch and release
To release fish back into the water unharmed as soon as they are caught.

corrode
To eat away at a metal through a chemical reaction.

dorsal fin
A fin on the top of a fish's back.

estuary
The spot where a sea's tide meets a river current.

harpoon
A spear used in hunting large fish.

inshore
Shallow coastal waters that are salt waters.

invasive species
A species that is not native to an environment and causes harm in that environment.

larval
Having to do with the young, wingless form of an insect after it hatches from an egg.

leader
A heavy piece of line that connects the main fishing line to the lure or hook.

offshore
In the ocean far from land.

reservoir
A human-made lake created when a dam is built on a river.

spawn
To release eggs and sperm into the water to reproduce.

spool
The part of a fishing reel that holds the fishing line.

surf
The waves of the sea that hit shore.

FURTHER READINGS

Carpenter, Tom. *Fishing*. Abdo, 2020.

Parker, Steve. *Eyewitness Fish*. DK, 2022.

Pembroke, Ethan. *The Shark Encyclopedia*. Abdo, 2021.

ONLINE RESOURCES

Booklinks
NONFICTION NETWORK
FREE! ONLINE NONFICTION RESOURCES

To learn more about fishing, please visit **abdobooklinks.com** or scan this QR code. These links are routinely monitored and updated to provide the most current information available.

INDEX

PHOTO CREDITS

ABDOBOOKS.COM

Published by Abdo Reference, a division of ABDO, PO Box 398166, Minneapolis, Minnesota 55439. Copyright © 2024 by Abdo Consulting Group, Inc. International copyrights reserved in all countries. No part of this book may be reproduced in any form without written permission from the publisher. Encyclopedias™ is a trademark and logo of Abdo Reference.

052023
092023

THIS BOOK CONTAINS
RECYCLED MATERIALS

Editor: Marie Pearson
Series Designer: Colleen McLaren
Production Designer: Michael J. Williams

LIBRARY OF CONGRESS CONTROL NUMBER: 2022949211

PUBLISHER'S CATALOGING-IN-PUBLICATION DATA
Names: McKinney, Donna B., author.
Title: The fishing encyclopedia / by Donna B. McKinney
Description: Minneapolis, Minnesota: Abdo Reference, 2024 | Series: Outdoor encyclopedias | Includes online resources and index.
Identifiers: ISBN 9781098291334 (lib. bdg.) | ISBN 9781098277512 (ebook)
Subjects: LCSH: Fishing--Juvenile literature. | Recreational fishing--Juvenile literature. | Sport fishing--Juvenile literature. | Encyclopedias and dictionaries--Juvenile literature.
Classification: DDC 796.5--dc23

WASHINGTON MIDDLE SCHOOL
314 SOUTH BAIRD STREET
GREEN BAY, WI 54301-3899